Ten Bed

Volu

ex libris

Candlestick Press

Published by:
Candlestick Press,
Diversity House, 72 Nottingham Road, Arnold, Nottingham NG5 6LF
www.candlestickpress.co.uk

Design, typesetting, print and production by Diversity Creative
Marketing Solutions Ltd., www.diversitymarketing.co.uk

Introduction and selection © Germaine Greer, 2015

Cover illustration © Judy Stevens, 2015
www.nbillustration.co.uk/judy-stevens

ISBN 978 1 907598 28 9

Candlestick Press wishes to thank Germaine Greer for her generosity.

Acknowledgements:
'Amo Ergo Sum' by Kathleen Raine appeared in *The Collected Poems
of Kathleen Raine*, Golgonooza Press, 2000, and is reprinted by kind
permission of the literary estate of Kathleen Raine, © 2000. In the
USA, W. H. Auden, 'Lullaby'(1937) copyright © 1940 and renewed
1968 by W.H. Auden, from W. H. Auden, *Collected Poems* is used by
permission of Random House, an imprint and division of Random
House LLC. All rights reserved. Any third party use of this material,
outside of this publication, is prohibited. Interested parties must apply
directly to Random House LLC for permission. Elsewhere,
W. H. Auden, 'Lullaby' from his *Collected Poems*, is reprinted by kind
permission of Curtis Brown, Ltd, © 1937.

Introduction

Poems are charms to be said rather than read. They need to be repeated like mantras before they can realise their full potency. When I was asked to produce a sampler of ten favourite bedtime poems, the surest way I had of coming up with a genuine list was to remember poems that dealt with bed and sleep – or lack of it – that I knew by heart. The ten that follow are all poems that English-speakers would be richer for knowing off by heart. Indeed, many people do already know them in whole or in part, which does not make them hackneyed, because they are the real thing. Their mystery and their meaning grow deeper, not shallower, every time we repeat them.

Most of my ten poems will be familiar; what may not be immediately apparent is that they are all connected to a tradition of poetry about sleep, a tradition so embedded that in 1816 21-year-old Keats could write a long poem called 'Poetry and Sleep'. Poets have always valued dreams and struggled to recreate them; the true bedtime poem is a doorway to the subconscious, an entry consciously and sometimes desperately sought. Dreaming is solitary but beds are also meeting-places. Bed is where we make most – and the most – of our love, and where we are most vividly aware of love lost.

My ten poems are all central to our poetic tradition, and so can be relied upon to fire the most multifarious of chain reactions. Yeats's 'Byzantium' should remind us of Coleridge's 'Kubla Khan', because it is orchestrated on the same scheme as that best-known of our dream-poems. 'Now sleeps the crimson petal, now the white…' from Tennyson's 'The Princess: A Medley', is a double bedtime poem; the Prince, the speaker of the whole poem, wakes up to hear Princess Ida reading it to herself 'deep in the night'.

Though I rather disapprove of 'excerpting' poems (because poems have shape as well as meaning, melody and rhythm), I have included a few stanzas from Byron's 'Don Juan'. This is the greatest comic poem in English and all too seldom read, partly because of the malign influence of Matthew Arnold and his insistence on high seriousness. Like most good comedy, 'Don Juan' is fundamentally serious, tragic even, and one of its great themes is the urgent need for the liberation of human sexuality. There is, besides, a tradition of poetry about the lovability of the beloved asleep; Auden was a great admirer of Byron whose spoor we can discern amid the pattern of Auden's 'Lullaby'.

I am well aware that only two of my ten poems are by women; all ten could have been by women but then the strength and breadth of the mainstream tradition would not have been discernible. Kathleen Raine's 'Amo Ergo Sum', a hymn of hope in which sleep and death, for centuries bedfellows in poetry, are reconciled, pays homage to that great tradition and takes its place within it.

Germaine Greer

Contents

A Complaint by Night of the Lover not Beloved

Alas! so all things now do hold their peace,
  Heaven and earth disturbèd in no thing.
The beasts, the air, the birds their song do cease;
  The night's car the stars about doth bring.
Calm is the sea – the waves work less and less –
  So am not I, whom love, alas, doth wring,
Bringing before my face the great increase
  Of my desires, whereat I weep and sing
In joy and woe, as in a doubtful ease,
  For my sweet thoughts sometime do pleasure bring
But by and by the cause of my disease
  Gives me a pang that inwardly doth sting,
When that I think what grief it is again
To live and lack the thing should rid my pain.

Henry Howard, Earl of Surrey (1517 - 1547)

Elegy XIX
To His Mistress Going To Bed

Come, Madam, come, all rest my powers defy;
Until I labour, I in labour lie.
The foe oft-times having the foe in sight,
Is tired with standing though he never fight.
Off with that girdle, like heaven's zone glistering,
But a far fairer world encompassing.
Unpin that spangled breastplate which you wear,
That the eyes of busy fools may be stopped there.
Unlace yourself, for that harmonious chime
Tells me from you, that now it is bed time.
Off with that happy busk, which I envy,
That still can be, and still can stand so nigh.
Your gown going off, such beauteous state reveals,
As when from flowery meads the hill's shadow steals.
Off with that wiry Coronet and shew
The hairy Diadem which on you doth grow.
Now off with those shoes, and then safely tread
In this love's hallow'd temple, this soft bed.
In such white robes, heaven's angels used to be
Received by men. Thou, angel, bringst with thee
A heaven like Mahomet's Paradise and, though
Ill spirits walk in white, we easily know
By this such angels from an evil sprite.
Those set our hairs but these our flesh upright.
    Licence my roving hands, and let them go,
Before, behind, between, above, below.
O my America! my new-found-land,
My kingdom, safeliest when with one man manned,
My mine of precious stones, my empiry,
How blest am I in thus discovering thee!
To enter in these bonds is to be free.
There, where my hand is set, my seal shall be.

Full nakedness, all joys are due to thee.
As souls unbodied, bodies unclothed must be
To taste whole joys. Gems which you women use
Are, like Atlanta's balls, cast in men's views
That, when a fool's eye lighteth on a gem,
His earthly soul may covet theirs, not them.
Like pictures or like books' gay coverings made
For lay-men are all women thus arrayed.
Themselves are mystic books, which only we
(Whom their imputed grace will dignify)
Must see revealed. Then, since that I may know,
As liberally as to a Midwife, shew
Thy self. Cast all, yea all this white linen hence,
There is no penance due to innocence.
　　To teach thee, I am naked first. Why then
What needst thou have more covering than a man?

John Donne (1572 – 1631)

Sonnet LXI

Is it thy will thy image should keep open
My heavy eyelids to the weary night?
Dost thou desire my slumbers should be broken,
While shadows, like to thee, do mock my sight?
Is it thy spirit that thou send'st from thee
So far from home into my deeds to pry,
To find out shames and idle hours in me,
The scope and tenor of thy jealousy?
O, no! thy love, though much, is not so great.
It is my love that keeps mine eye awake,
Mine own true love that doth my rest defeat,
To play the watchman ever for thy sake.
   For thee watch I whilst thou dost wake elsewhere,
   From me far off, with others all too near.

William Shakespeare (1564 – 1616)

A Nocturnal Reverie

In such a night, when every louder wind
Is to its distant cavern safe confined;
And only gentle Zephyr fans his wings,
And lonely Philomel, still waking, sings;
Or from some tree, famed for the owl's delight,
She, hollowing clear, directs the wand'rer right:
In such a night, when passing clouds give place,
Or thinly veil the heav'ns' mysterious face;
When in some river, overhung with green,
The waving moon and the trembling leaves are seen;
When freshened grass now bears itself upright,
And makes cool banks to pleasing rest invite,
Whence springs the woodbind, and the bramble-rose,
And where the sleepy cowslip sheltered grows;
Whilst now a paler hue the foxglove takes,
Yet checkers still with red the dusky brakes
When scatter'd glow-worms, but in twilight fine,
Shew trivial beauties, watch their hour to shine;
Whilst Salisb'ry stands the test of every light,
In perfect charms, and perfect virtue bright:
When odors, which declined repelling day,
Through temp'rate air uninterrupted stray;
When darkened groves their softest shadows wear,
And falling waters we distinctly hear;
When through the gloom more venerable shows
Some ancient fabric, awful in repose,
While sunburnt hills their swarthy looks conceal,
And swelling haycocks thicken up the vale:

When the loosed horse now, as his pasture leads,
Comes slowly grazing through th' adjoining meads,
Whose stealing pace, and lengthened shade we fear,
Till torn-up forage in his teeth we hear:
When nibbling sheep at large pursue their food,
And unmolested kine rechew the cud;
When curlews cry beneath the village walls,
And to her straggling brood the partridge calls;
Their shortlived jubilee the creatures keep,
Which but endures, whilst tyrant man does sleep;
When a sedate content the spirit feels,
And no fierce light disturbs, whilst it reveals;
But silent musings urge the mind to seek
Something, too high for syllables to speak;
Till the free soul to a composedness charmed,
Finding the elements of rage disarmed,
O'er all below a solemn quiet grown,
Joys in th' inferior world, and thinks it like her own:
In such a night let me abroad remain,
Till morning breaks, and all's confused again;
Our cares, our toils, our clamors are renewed,
Or pleasures, seldom reached, again pursued.

Anne Finch, Countess of Winchilsea (1661 – 1720)

from Don Juan, Canto II

They look upon each other, and their eyes
　　Gleam in the moonlight; and her white arm clasps
Round Juan's head, and his around her lies
　　Half buried in the tresses which it grasps;
She sits upon his knee, and drinks his sighs,
　　He hers, until they end in broken gasps;
And thus they form a group that's quite antique,
Half naked, loving, natural, and Greek.

And when those deep and burning moments pass'd,
　　And Juan sunk to sleep within her arms,
She slept not, but all tenderly, though fast,
　　Sustain'd his head upon her bosom's charms;
And now and then her eye to heaven is cast,
　　And then on the pale cheek her breast now warms,
Pillow'd on her o'erflowing heart, which pants
With all it granted, and with all it grants.

An infant when it gazes on a light,
　　A child the moment when it drains the breast,
A devotee when soars the Host in sight,
　　An Arab with a stranger for a guest,
A sailor when the prize has struck in fight,
　　A miser filling his most hoarded chest,
Feel rapture; but not such true joy are reaping
As they who watch o'er what they love while sleeping.

For there it lies so tranquil, so beloved,
  All that it hath of life with us is living;
So gentle, stirless, helpless, and unmoved,
  And all unconscious of the joy't is giving;
All it hath felt, inflicted, pass'd, and proved,
  Hush'd into depths beyond the watcher's diving:
There lies the thing we love with all its errors
And all its charms, like death without its terrors.

George Gordon (Lord) Byron (1788 – 1824)

To Sleep

A flock of sheep that leisurely pass by
One after one; the sound of rain, and bees
Murmuring; the fall of rivers, winds and seas,
Smooth fields, white sheets of water, and pure sky,
I've thought of all by turns, and still I lie
Sleepless; and soon the small birds' melodies
Must hear, first utter'd from my orchard trees,
And the first cuckoo's melancholy cry.
Even thus last night, and two nights more I lay,
And could not win thee, Sleep! by any stealth;
So do not let me wear tonight away.
Without thee what is all the morning's wealth?
Come, blessed barrier between day and day,
Dear mother of fresh thoughts and joyous health!

William Wordsworth (1770 – 1850)

Sonnet from **The Princess: A Medley**

Now sleeps the crimson petal, now the white;
Nor waves the cypress in the palace walk;
Nor winks the gold fin in the porphyry font:
The firefly wakens: waken thou with me.

Now droops the milkwhite peacock like a ghost,
And like a ghost she glimmers on to me.

Now lies the Earth all Danaë to the stars,
And all thy heart lies open unto me.

Now slides the silent meteor on, and leaves
A shining furrow, as thy thoughts in me.

Now folds the lily all her sweetness up,
And slips into the bosom of the lake:
So fold thyself, my dearest, thou, and slip
Into my bosom and be lost in me.

Alfred (Lord) Tennyson (1809 – 1892)

Byzantium

The unpurged images of day recede;
The Emperor's drunken soldiery are abed;
Night resonance recedes, night-walkers' song
After great cathedral gong;
A starlit or a moonlit dome disdains
All that man is,
All mere complexities,
The fury and the mire of human veins.

Before me floats an image, man or shade,
Shade more than man, more image than a shade;
For Hades' bobbin bound in mummy-cloth
May unwind the winding path;
A mouth that has no moisture and no breath
Breathless mouths may summon;
I hail the superhuman;
I call it death-in-life and life-in-death.

Miracle, bird or golden handiwork,
More miracle than bird or handiwork,
Planted on the starlit golden bough,
Can like the cocks of Hades crow,
Or, by the moon embittered, scorn aloud
In glory of changeless metal
Common bird or petal
And all complexities of mire or blood.

At midnight on the Emperor's pavement flit
Flames that no faggot feeds, nor steel has lit,
Nor storm disturbs, flames begotten of flame,
Where blood-begotten spirits come
And all complexities of fury leave,
Dying into a dance,
An agony of trance,
An agony of flame that cannot singe a sleeve.

Astraddle on the dolphin's mire and blood,
Spirit after spirit! The smithies break the flood,
The golden smithies of the Emperor!
Marbles of the dancing floor
Break bitter furies of complexity,
Those images that yet
Fresh images beget,
That dolphin-torn, that gong-tormented sea.

William Butler Yeats (1865 – 1939)

Lullaby

Lay your sleeping head, my love,
Human on my faithless arm;
Time and fevers burn away
Individual beauty from
Thoughtful children, and the grave
Proves the child ephemeral:
But in my arms till break of day
Let the living creature lie,
Mortal, guilty, but to me
The entirely beautiful.

Soul and body have no bounds:
To lovers as they lie upon
Her tolerant enchanted slope
In their ordinary swoon,
Grave the vision Venus sends
Of supernatural sympathy,
Universal love and hope;
While an abstract insight wakes
Among the glaciers and the rocks
The hermit's sensual ecstasy.

Certainty, fidelity
On the stroke of midnight pass
Like vibrations of a bell,
And fashionable madmen raise
Their pedantic boring cry:
Every farthing of the cost,
All the dreaded cards foretell,
Shall be paid, but not from this night
Not a whisper, not a thought,
Not a kiss nor look be lost.

Beauty, midnight, vision dies:
Let the winds of dawn that blow
Softly round your dreaming head
Such a day of sweetness show
Eye and knocking heart may bless,
Find the mortal world enough;
Noons of dryness see you fed
By the involuntary powers,
Nights of insult let you pass
Watched by every human love.

W. H. Auden (1907 – 1973)

Amo Ergo Sum

Because I love
    The sun pours out its rays of living gold
    Pours out its gold and silver on the sea.

Because I love
    The earth upon her astral spindle winds
    Her ecstasy-producing dance.

Because I love
    Clouds travel on the winds through wide skies,
    Skies wide and beautiful, blue and deep.

Because I love
    Wind blows white sails,
    The wind blows over flowers, the sweet wind blows.

Because I love
    The ferns grow green, and green the grass, and green
    The transparent sunlit trees.

Because I love
    Larks rise up from the grass
    And all the leaves are full of singing birds.

Because I love
    The summer air quivers with a thousand wings,
    Myriads of jewelled eyes burn in the light.

Because I love
    The iridescent shells upon the sand
    Take forms as fine and intricate as thought.

Because I love
    There is an invisible way across the sky,
    Birds travel by that way, the sun and moon
    And all the stars travel that path by night.

Because I love
    There is a river flowing all night long.

Because I love
    All night the river flows into my sleep,
    Ten thousand living things are sleeping in my arms,
    And sleeping wake, and flowing are at rest.

Kathleen Raine (1908 - 2003)